On helping
the dyslexic child

On helping
the dyslexic child

T. R. MILES

METHUEN EDUCATIONAL LTD

LONDON · TORONTO · SYDNEY · WELLINGTON

First published 1970
by Methuen Educational Ltd
11 New Fetter Lane, London EC4P 4EE
Reprinted 1971, 1972, 1974, 1977

© *1970 T. R. Miles*

Printed in Great Britain by
Lowe & Brydone Printers Limited, Thetford, Norfolk

ISBN 0 423 43070 X Cased
     0 423 43080 7 Paper

Distributed in the USA by
HARPER & ROW PUBLISHERS, INC
BARNES & NOBLE IMPORT DIVISION

Contents

Preface

Although quite a large amount has been written on the theoretical aspects of dyslexia, little has been published on the day-to-day problems of helping the dyslexic child. The aim of this booklet is essentially a practical one, and I have deliberately kept the theoretical issues in the background except in so far as they are relevant to problems of practical handling.

Unfortunately, however, the whole subject of dyslexia has produced considerable controversy, some of it extremely heated; and it is perhaps appropriate, therefore, to make some kind of personal statement at the start. I myself am in no doubt that the term *dyslexia* (or some word of equivalent meaning) is a necessity if certain sorts of backward readers and spellers are to be adequately helped. It is simply not true, in my experience, that parents are demoralised or discouraged when they are told that their child is dyslexic. On the contrary, surprising as it may seem, they are often very much relieved. The reason, I think, is that, when information about dyslexia is given, this makes sense of what would otherwise have seemed utterly bewildering. I have often met parents who could tell that *something* was wrong, without knowing what; and if one can make clear that the child is suffering from a recognised disability about which certain fairly probable predictions can be made, this enables them to come to a realistic appraisal of the difficulties which they and the child will have to face. Similarly, if teachers can be told, not 'Here is yet another backward speller,' but rather, 'Here is a backward speller *with a disability which requires special understanding*,' it will be far easier for them to help the child in a constructive way.

If this were a purely theoretical issue there would be little justification for heated argument. In practice, however, my experience is that, when the value of the term *dyslexia* has been disputed or not recognised, the result has often been an appalling failure even to appreciate what the problems of these children are, let alone to press for adequate remedial facilities. Too often in the past so-called 'experts' have caused unnecessary worry in both parents and children by assuming that the more intractable difficulties in reading and spelling are the result of the child's fears and anxieties about human relationships in the family. The term *dyslexia* seems to me to mark a noteworthy advance on this traditional view, since it implies that one should look instead for difficulties in the retention of shapes and sounds and that these difficulties should be treated in their own right, not as symptoms of underlying emotional disturbance. Certainly I have come across occasional children who were disturbed or difficult as well as being weak at reading and spelling; but where the diagnosis of dyslexia is correct there is a good chance that the anti-social behaviour will disappear when the anxieties over reading and spelling are alleviated. This can be achieved not by traditional psychotherapy nor even by sympathy and kindness—at any rate not by these on their own—but by a genuine attempt on the part of the remedial teacher to understand what the child cannot do and to offer him means of overcoming his difficulty. The inference from 'This child has not responded to ordinary teaching methods' to 'Therefore his failure must be due to emotional disturbance' seems to me highly dubious.

To parents and teachers who find themselves being given contradictory information from different sources as to whether a condition called *dyslexia* exists, my suggestion would be: do not worry too much about the name, but make sure the child is in the hands of someone who is determined to understand where his difficulties lie.

On the theoretical side I am quite willing to agree that what is involved may be better described as a family of disabilities rather than as a single condition; but it seems to me that there is sufficient similarity in the behaviour-patterns of dyslexic children to justify tentative generalisations from one case to another. Although there is much that we do not know, it does not follow that we know nothing at all.

Having said this, I should like to emphasise the limited nature of what is being attempted in the present booklet. My purpose is simply to make some of my experience with dyslexic children available to those interested. I do not claim any novelty for the teaching methods advocated; indeed I am not suggesting that dyslexic children should be taught by one method and one only. What I am offering is a personal selection from the many techniques now available. The suggestions made here are in fact ones which I myself have found useful in intermittent coaching sessions over a period of nearly twenty years. During this time I have been concerned not with mildly backward children but with children having really severe difficulties over reading and spelling, children for whom the ordinary class conditions and even 'extra tuition' have proved inadequate.

So many different factors have been involved in this work that any statistics of 'success-rate' would, I am sure, be misleading rather than informative. In particular a high 'success-rate' might simply mean that I had been teaching some of the milder cases. Quite apart from this, however, the use of statistical tables in the present context would imply that there exists one single teaching method in isolation, whereas it seems to me that what is needed for dyslexic children is the skilful blending of a variety of methods. What I am offering, therefore, should be regarded as a series of suggestions, not as a set of inflexible rules, and it will be for the teacher to adapt them in accordance with the needs of the individual child.

I should like to thank Mrs Sandhya Naidoo, Director of the Word Blind Centre for Dyslexic Children, who has read the booklet in the original typescript and made many helpful suggestions. I have also learned a great deal from others associated with the Centre, in particular Dr A. White Franklin, Dr Macdonald Critchley, and Miss G. C. Cotterell, though none of them is responsible for what is contained here. Finally I should like to acknowledge a long-standing debt of gratitude to Professor O. L. Zangwill who first aroused my interest in dyslexia and who has given me continual encouragement in this field over many years.

Bangor, 1970   T R M

CHAPTER ONE

What to look for

Among children who are weak at reading and spelling those suffering from dyslexia form a special group. I should like to begin by indicating how one can pick out the dyslexic child and how he or she* differs from other poor readers and spellers.

Perhaps the most useful starting-point is to consider whether one can exclude more straightforward explanations of the child's difficulties. Thus plenty of children are weak at reading and spelling simply because it is not easy for them to deal with intellectual tasks in general. In such cases the term *dyslexia* would be entirely inappropriate. What we need to be on the look out for is a special weakness which displays itself in reading and spelling (or in some cases in spelling only), when in many other respects the child does not behave like a dullard at all. For example, most dyslexic children (not all of them) are able to cope with arithmetic; many of them can learn by heart with no difficulty, and most can follow highly complex reasoning, even though they cannot put the correct answer on paper. One of the pioneers in this area, Hinshelwood, describes the pathetic story of a child who learned his reading book by heart and thus for some time avoided detection when he was required to read in front of the class.† It is not impossible for a child to be dyslexic as well as dull, but if he is weak all round you

* Throughout this booklet I shall for brevity use 'he' rather than the more cumbersome 'he or she'. The condition is in fact more common among boys; but what I say should normally be understood as applying to girls no less than boys. For discussion of sex differences see M. Critchley (1970), p. 91 and J. Money (ed.) (1962), p. 31. Details of both these books are given on p. 67.

† My source is J. Hinshelwood, *Congenital Word Blindness*, London 1917, p. 45.

would have no special reason for suspecting the presence of dyslexia.

Again, if a child is known to have undergone some particularly unpleasant shock, e.g. the death of a parent, or to have had to tolerate other difficulties at home, you might find that his performance at reading and spelling suffered (particularly if he was of an age, say under eight, when these skills had not been fully learned). In such a case, however, you would probably find that his school work was affected as a whole, and that the failure was not limited to reading and spelling. Although it is of course perfectly possible for a dyslexic child to have other worries in his life, you would have no good reason for suspecting dyslexia if the child's failure could be explained in these other terms.

The same holds in the case of absence from school. A bright child who had been absent might find difficulty with reading and spelling when he later returned to his class; but the obvious explanation of the failure would in this case be the absences. Similarly, if you know that a particular school or a particular class notoriously fails in teaching children to read and spell, and one of your children had recently come from such a class or school, you would probably be right to attribute his failure to poor teaching.

You may occasionally meet cases where failure at reading or spelling is due to defective eyesight or hearing. Thus even a child who has had a thorough medical check may have lost his glasses or for some reason be unable or unwilling to use them; and it is conceivable that slight hearing loss could go undetected.

Children who have suffered from any of these handicaps clearly merit attention and sympathy; but their needs are different from those of the dyslexic child.

If, however, the child's failure has been limited to a few specific areas (including reading and spelling in particular) and if this failure cannot be explained along the lines indicated above—if, one might say, there is something genuinely *puzzling* about the child's failure, something which *does not make sense* —then one possibility, among others, is that the child is dyslexic. At this stage it is worth-while looking for some of the positive signs.

One of the most important of these is confusion over direction. This can take various forms, for example misreading *b* for *d* or *p* for *q*, or making the corresponding mistake in writing them. Thus one boy whom I taught confused *boys* with *dogs*, and recently I have come across *tolq* for *tulip* and *catqil* for *caterpillar*. Sometimes the letters of a word are in the wrong order, e.g. *dna* for *and*. You should not, of course, take mistakes of this kind too seriously when they are made by five- and six-year-olds; they are very common in the early stages of learning to read and write, and the great majority of children grow out of them by the age of seven or eight at the latest. If the child is to be diagnosed as dyslexic, one would need evidence of *persistent* difficulties over direction, continuing up to the age of nine, ten or beyond; and one sometimes finds that, even though the final mark on the paper is the right way round, say *b* and not *d*, there has been an enormous expenditure of effort to achieve this. The crossings out in their exercise books repay detailed study. In particular, care is often needed in trying to discover whether the child has genuinely made a directional mistake (as would be the case, for instance, if he wrote *dna* for *and*—a correct spelling apart from a systematic confusion of the 'back-to-front' variety) or whether he simply did not know what letter to put next; thus it is not clear out of context whether a child who writes *whte* for *with* is making a 'back-to-front' mistake over the *t-h* or whether he is simply relying on guesswork and vague memories.

Occasionally, too, there is confusion in the vertical plane, as when *h* is confused with *y*, but I have found this less common than horizontal confusions such as *b-d* and *p-q*. In what follows I shall refer to those mistakes over the direction of letters and words as *reversals*. (In the more technical literature you may come across the word *strephosymbolia*. This amounts to precisely the same thing. It means literally 'turning of symbols', and it seems to me a harmless enough word apart from being something of a 'mouthful'.)

WEAHFR

When water comes a lot of vapor it is
had or different do make a Sudden with
say Soda water is known heed

Sample 1

Dain

    I am written to in a bat the next set.
then at prof at the show clopat subban. Now
even you get in from your from you practise
the root of yres.

          Yours etc-

Sample 2

[handwritten] one day feart chilin went
to rog theymother wech will.
we b going for nw hotday

One day five children went to ask their mother, Where shall we be going for our
holiday?

[handwritten] W en a oled sepedns lwziis it
on from, and is adsorned in a lineced,
we ser the sopsts has drorend in
the lweewed.

When a solid substance loses its own form, and is absorbed in a liquid, we say the
substance has dissolved in the liquid.

5

Often the spelling is very strange in appearance. (For illustrations see pages 4–5.)

Both the examples on page 4 were copied from school exercise books; as I was not present at the time I am unsure what the child was trying to say. On page 5, however, are two further examples where, despite the oddity, it is possible to decipher the child's intentions with some degree of confidence.

Although not all dyslexic children spell as strangely as this, these extreme examples illustrate in a particularly instructive way where the main difficulty often lies. I should like to emphasise that the boys who produced these spellings all came out above average on standard intelligence tests, the boy who was responsible for sample 4 being right up in the 'superior' range. How, then, can children of undisputed ability write such utter nonsense?

The point, as I see it, is that although *to us* these efforts are nonsense, to the children themselves they are no more and no less nonsense than most other marks on paper. Indeed once the complexity of the total shape reaches more than a certain amount, the distinction between what is nonsense and what is meaningful does not arise for them. From bitter experience a child may well expect to be told that some or all of his words are wrongly spelled, but he has no means of telling for himself which of them are wrong or why they are wrong. There is— one is tempted to say—a certain *blindness* a. recognising words, not because the child is blind in the ordinary sense, but because the marks on paper somehow do not 'click'. An old name for dyslexia was *word-blindness*—a somewhat curious term perhaps, but still informative, in my opinion, since it suggests that in some curious way there is something which the child just cannot *see*, even though in the ordinary sense his vision may be perfectly normal.

As a result of his disability the child is in no position to 'monitor' what he has written. His only choice is to use such cues as he can (including extraneous ones such as the expression on the teacher's face!). One obvious device is to pay attention to his own mouth-movements when he says the word. The fact that much of the spelling of dyslexic children is phonetic in character suggests that this is what they have been doing. Some of the errors are precisely those where differences in mouth-movements are not sufficient to be noticed. Thus when *substance* in sample 4 is spelled as *sepedns* and *sopsts*, one of the errors involved is confusion between *b* and *p*, presumably because they are phonetically similar. Also this particular boy often had special difficulty in knowing what vowel to put (*soled* for *solid* is an example), and I do not doubt that this was due to the difficulty in distinguishing the different mouth-movements for different vowel sounds. Again, the *feouf* (for *five*) in sample 3 involves, among other things, the substitution of a second *f* where there should in fact be a *v*; here, too, it is a case where two letters, *f* and *v*, have similar mouth-movements and are therefore not distinguished.

Their spelling is often further complicated by acquired knowledge and vague memories. Thus sample 2, if my interpretation is correct, starts: 'I am writing to you about . . .'. For this boy *un* is not a foolish attempt at *you*. He continually used to leave out the *n* in words such as *found* and *ground*, and had often been corrected over this; and he may well have been aware that, despite the sound, one cannot spell *you* as simply *u*; he therefore brought in the extra *n* because he remembered that in some contexts an extra *n* was needed. This, incidentally, is quite compatible with his *correct* spelling of *you* in the third line. It is perfectly possible for dyslexic children to remember a word correctly on one occasion or in one context and not on another.

In the absence of any recognition of visual absurdity, *on*, in sample 4, is a perfectly plausible attempt at *own*, and in sample 3 *rsg* is a perfectly plausible attempt at *ask*. I do not claim that *all* misspellings by dyslexic children can be understood along these lines, since it is perfectly possible that sometimes the child in his despair will simply make a wild 'shot'; but I am sure that there is a great deal more method in their efforts than there appears to be at first glance.

Other points of interest in sample 4 are: *ist* for *its* (a directional confusion), the substitution of *d* for *b* in *absorbed*, and the

7

two different spellings of *substance* (*sepedns* and *sopsts*) and of *liquid* (*lwecae* and *lwecwed*).

The spelling which results when a child cannot monitor what he has written I propose to call *bizarre* spelling. You can take it as firmly established that bizarre spelling and reversals commonly go together.

A further complication requires mention at this point. It has been my experience that, when a dyslexic child begins to overcome his disabilities, his reading starts to improve sooner than his spelling. Indeed you may come across children who, though weak at spelling, can read quite fluently. I think that one would still be justified in calling such children *dyslexic*, provided that at an earlier age there had been some evidence both of reading disability and of the related signs such as confusion over direction. The practical decision in such cases is whether their spelling is sufficiently weak that it still requires special coaching, or whether the child would be better off if he simply returned to his normal class.

Here are some additional signs of dyslexia, though they do not occur in every case. Sometimes the handwriting is curiously awkward, as in the case of sample 1. Sometimes the child is reported as being clumsy in his movements,* and in some cases there is evidence of speech difficulties. It has also been suggested that dyslexic children are more likely than other children to show ill-defined handedness, in the sense of not being clearly right-handed or clearly left-handed. In addition I have known some dyslexic children who completely failed-at giving rhymes; I do not mean merely that they could not, for example, say *cat* if asked to give a rhyme for *bat*, but that they did not seem to have the least idea what a rhyme was. Quite a number of them have difficulty in copying abstract shapes and designs. In many cases they cannot recognise a word even though they have been shown it a few moments before. Some of them have difficulty in repeating longer words orally without getting the syllables in the wrong order; in the case of more intelligent children you

* When I recently examined the records of thirty-eight dyslexic children, I found a report of clumsiness in ten cases.

may like to test them with awkward words such as *discrimination* and *preliminary*.

To sum up: a dyslexic child is one who has special difficulty with spelling and usually with reading also, his performance falling a long way short of his intellectual level. Often he continues to *reverse* letters and words at an age when other children no longer do so, and his spelling is frequently *bizarre* in the sense described earlier in this chapter. In some cases there are the additional signs mentioned in the previous paragraph. Whenever you come across a child who fits this general picture, you would be right to label him as a *dyslexic*, and to realise that his problems merit special attention.

A concluding note. The use of standardised tests

If there is any doubt as to a child's general ability or level of educational attainment, arrangements can be made for him to take standardised tests. In this context I am thinking in particular of intelligence tests and tests of reading and spelling. When a test has been standardised, this means that it has been given to a large number of children—probably thousands—and that figures are available which show what is the average or expected performance for children of a given age. On the basis of the results you can then tell how far a particular child is above or below the average.

In the case of dyslexic children, however, various cautions are necessary. Thus, in trying to reach an assessment of the intellectual level of a dyslexic child, one needs to remember that there are items in traditional intelligence tests which cannot be correctly answered unless the child can read the instructions; dyslexic children may therefore fail the item not because it is too difficult intellectually, but simply because of their reading difficulty. Also some test-items demand ability to handle various abstract kinds of spatial relationship, and, in these cases, if a dyslexic child fails, this may be simply an indication of his special disability, not an indication of lack of intelligence. A simple adding up of correct answers is therefore likely to give a false picture. Consequently, if you have been told the IQ figure for a dyslexic child, you would, I am sure, be wise to treat it with caution; and if you are familiar with intelligence tests in general, you may find it helpful to obtain precise information as to which test-items he passed and failed. If he has been successful in some very difficult items, this should certainly be taken seriously, even if he has failed some of the easier ones; and in general it seems to me that you would be right to regard a high score as an important piece of evidence, even if in the case of a low score you decide to reserve judgment.

In addition to intelligence tests one can also give the child tests of attainment at reading and spelling. If the child is a long way behind the average for his age, the problem of remedial education becomes all the more urgent. As with intelligence tests, however, one should not regard the total score as more than a rough guide. It should be remembered that, when a child is required in these tests to read or spell a word, each particular answer is counted simply as 'right' or 'wrong'; in the case of dyslexic children, however, it is often desirable not simply to note the total score (which may sometimes even be misleading) but in addition to study the *kinds* of mistake which they have made and to work out in detail what they find difficult.

The main advantage of using standardised tests is that one is then in a position to compare a child's attainment at reading and spelling with his intellectual level. It does not, of course, follow that all children who show a discrepancy between intelligence and attainment are dyslexic, but where such a discrepancy is accompanied by some of the other signs which I have described, one can diagnose *dyslexia* with a high degree of confidence.

CHAPTER TWO

The causes of dyslexia

The causes of dyslexia are not known for certain. Personally I am in no doubt that, where children display the pattern of disabilities described in the previous chapter, it is right to think in terms of something constitutional—something, that is, associated with the physical constitution of the child; in particular it would seem that somehow or other there are some slight abnormalities in the way in which the brain has developed. Beyond this, however, one cannot go with any degree of certainty.

I have met few cases where there was any history of an accident severe enough to suggest that the brain has actually been damaged during childhood. Occasionally there are reports of difficulty at birth, but these are the exception rather than the rule. In general—and in so far as one can distinguish the two—it seems to me that one should talk not so much of damage as of failure of development. Moreover, since the brain is continually changing in all sorts of ways, it does not follow that such failure will be permanent.

Some investigators have wondered if there is an inherited factor at work, and there are certainly cases on record where more than one member of a family has been affected. Precisely what brain mechanisms are involved, however, is not known for certain, and it may quite well be that dyslexia results when there is a *combination* of adverse factors. It may even be that the causes are different in different cases.

If children or parents have a garbled idea of what is happening (e.g. 'my last teacher said there was something queer about my brain'), you will be doing a kind act if you put them right. The sort of thing which I have sometimes said to parents is, 'He is perfectly all right in other respects but there is just some small failure of brain development, and this makes it difficult for him to recognise shapes and letters.'

The brain abnormalities, if they exist, are, of course, very slight, and one should always bear in mind the enormous number of things which dyslexic children can do perfectly well.

For practical purposes it does not seem to me that a knowledge of the details of what causes dyslexia is necessary. What I believe to be important (though perhaps not all educational psychologists would agree with me) is the recognition that dyslexia is a special variety of the condition known in medical books as 'aphasia'. This is a condition which sometimes occurs in adults as a result of brain injury, and the effect of it is that they sometimes become confused in their speech and thinking. Here is an example:* a patient is presented with two sticks $\vee\!\!\!/$ and is required to copy them; he cannot do so. When presented with a different pattern, however, *viz* $\wedge$, he can copy them with no difficulty. When asked how this is so, he says that the second pattern is a roof whereas the first is 'nothing'. Sometimes adult aphasic patients can read a few familiar words but cannot cope with unfamiliar material; and when a certain area of the brain is damaged—the fronto-parietal area—although they may be able to find their way about their home or the hospital, they may have difficulty in *representing* home or hospital if required to make a plan drawing. In general there is quite often a difficulty in coping with symbolic or abstract material and in particular with putting the parts in the right order.

The analogy with aphasia seems to me relevant for the following reasons. **i** One can say, as a result, that the dyslexic child's disability is no one's fault—neither that of the parent for being incompetent, unloving, over-protective, neurotic, etc, nor that of the teacher for failing to teach properly. **ii** One can appreciate that the child is handicapped, just as, for instance, a lame child is handicapped, even if the handicap in this case is less spectacular and obvious. **iii** One can learn to make sense of the mistakes which these children make by comparing these

* My source is K. Goldstein, *On Human Nature*, New York 1963, p. 41.

mistakes with those made by aphasic adults. Thus one would expect all dyslexic children to be able to recognise, say, a picture of an elephant, since little by way of abstraction is involved; but one would expect many of them to have difficulty over making or interpreting the symbolic marks on paper which constitute the written word 'elephant', and one would expect some of them to have difficulty in repeating longer words since this involves putting the syllables in the right order.
iv Where there is something that the child definitely cannot do (e.g. recognise words at sight), it seems to me more sensible to offer him a way round his disability than to press him to 'keep trying', since the brain mechanisms necessary for success by that particular method may simply not be there. (It is, of course, quite conceivable that such mechanisms may develop a few years later, and this possibility should certainly be examined in the case of older children where there is a history of earlier failure; but in general my experience is that encouraging the child in what he *can* do is better than urging him to practise those things which he *cannot* do.) I think that all those who have thoroughly studied the mistakes made by dyslexic children would agree that the analogy with aphasia is worth taking seriously.

To sum up: it seems to me that one is right to think of dyslexia as a variety of aphasia, that is, as an inability to handle and order symbolic or abstract material. The causes are not known in detail, but the condition is almost certainly connected with some small failure of development in the brain.

CHAPTER THREE

The decision to try to help

Let us begin with the situation where you yourself suspect that a child is dyslexic, but where the question has not been raised by anyone else. Since the condition is still not at all widely recognised, this may quite well happen.

Your first move will presumably be to get a second opinion —from a colleague, perhaps, from the school medical officer, or from an educational psychologist. Even if they do not share all the views on dyslexia which I am putting forward here, they will be almost sure to agree that special coaching is needed. At a suitable point it will of course be necessary to consult the parents. The basic problem is likely to be that of finding a suitable teacher. This may well not be easy, since although there may be people available who have had experience of remedial teaching in general, you will find very few indeed with specialist experience of dyslexic children. At present there is danger that those suffering from dyslexia may be put in a class with children who are failing at school for quite other reasons. This is disastrous. For the bright dyslexic child an 'ordinary' class is too difficult, a 'backward' class quite unsuitable; and one hopes that more provision will be made in the future for bright children with reading and spelling disabilities.

It is small comfort, then, to be told to look for a specialist teacher. Yet to do nothing at all for the child will almost certainly be the least satisfactory solution. This means that the only choice left is that the child should be taught by someone, however inexperienced, who is willing to try to learn more. This could be you.

Let us be quite realistic about this. You will be undertaking a very difficult assignment; progress may be very slow indeed, particularly in the early stages, and both you and the child may well find the situation very frustrating. I am not saying this to discourage you, but it seems to me important that you should make this decision with your eyes open and that neither you nor the child should expect too much too soon.

It is even possible, if you are a parent, that you may consider attempting to do the teaching yourself. Whether this is a good idea may vary from one family to another. In this connection I cannot help being reminded of the situation where a husband teaches his wife to drive a car; this works in some cases and not in others! I am certainly not opposed in principle to the idea of parental tuition for dyslexic children, provided that the responsibility is genuinely shared and that both the child and the parents are prepared for a hard slog. It is perhaps less easy for a parent than for an outsider to strike the right balance between pressing the child too hard and not pressing him hard enough, and if the child feels that his parents do not understand his difficulties, this is likely to be more distressing to him than if there is lack of understanding from someone outside the family. These objections, however, are not insuperable, and in general it seems to me to be a matter which families must decide for themselves.

Where parents can certainly help is in reading aloud. There must of necessity be many dyslexic children for whom reading to themselves has never been a pleasure, since it has always involved an enormous expenditure of effort. As a result, it seems likely that many are unaware of the large amount of enjoyment to be derived from books. One needs to remember the extent to which all weak readers are cut off from pleasures which other children enjoy; I am thinking here not only of adventure stories and biographies, but of magazines and newspapers, of captions on television, and even of instruction manuals. (Imagine the child who is longing to assemble the parts of a toy aeroplane and cannot read what he is supposed to do!) If parents and others read aloud to these children, all sorts of exciting pleasures become available which they would otherwise have missed.

Also, if you are a parent, do not hesitate to press for help. This will be to the good of all dyslexic children in the long run, and I am sure that the great majority of those whom you approach will be sympathetic. If occasionally you come across people who say or imply that you are over-fussy, do not be discouraged. If your child is genuinely dyslexic, then those who fail to take your problem seriously are simply revealing their own ignorance.

Here are a few more points of a general kind. If you are a teacher, doctor or psychologist and have occasion to mention the word *dyslexia* to parents or to the child himself, there is no need to put on a long face or speak as if it were some terrible or unmentionable calamity. Dyslexia is a handicap which, unless treated, will restrict the child's opportunities. To say less is to be unrealistic, certainly; but to say more is to be unnecessarily alarmist. It seems to me perfectly possible when talking to the child himself to explain that he is likely to have more difficulty with reading and spelling than do other children; after all he almost certainly knows this already! If it is clear to parents and child that nothing is being kept back, this will itself be a source of reassurance.

The sort of information which I myself usually give to parents is as follows. 1 This is a peculiar difficulty which some children have, and which requires special teaching. 2 It has only recently become at all widely recognised. 3 We do not know the cause, but there appears to be some small part of the brain which has not quite developed properly. 4 Although one needs to be cautious, there is some evidence which suggests that the disability runs in families. 5 It is not the child's fault that he has this disability, nor is it the fault of his teachers that they have not been able to teach him. 6 Even with special teaching the going will be hard; for instance the child may not be able to read a word which was shown to him a few moments previously. (This may in fact be something which the parents have already noticed, and it may well be reassuring to them to know that it is a recognised part of dyslexia.) 7 One cannot be sure of the outcome, and the child may always find spelling difficult, but there is a good chance of getting him to the stage where he can read for pleasure and write intelligibly with the aid of a dictionary.

If the parents put questions to you other than those which can be answered along those lines, it is perfectly reasonable to say that you do not know.

One further question may arise: how long will it be necessary for the child to receive extra remedial help? Much will depend on the degree of severity, but as a rough guide one should perhaps think in terms of a period of one to two years. If possible the child should come for several sessions per week, and I do not think sessions should last for more than about fifty minutes. Sometimes, because of travelling difficulties, there is no option but to limit the child to one session per week, but in the more severe cases this may be too little.

Finally, one needs to bear in mind the problem in so far as it affects the parents. Dyslexia falls on families of all different types. Some dyslexic children are worriers, some are difficult and obstinate, some—apart from the handicap of dyslexia—are perfectly happy. Similarly some parents are worriers, and some, perhaps, do not worry sufficiently. In any case, it is not easy, I am sure, for those who have a dyslexic child to view the situation with realism. This means you are likely to meet anxiety on the part of such parents, and in some cases you may even meet hostility and aggression. Such behaviour is understandable, and they need your sympathy.

CHAPTER FOUR

Some suggested guide-lines

Let us suppose that you have decided to take on a dyslexic child for remedial teaching and that you are wondering how best to help him.

On helping the dyslexic child

I should like in the first place to emphasise the *limitations* of this booklet. In particular I do not want to give the impression that success can be achieved simply by following a set of instructions. In what follows I shall try to indicate some of the points which I myself have found helpful. My purpose, however, is not to 'tell you how it ought to be done' but to give you ideas. If what I say can be adapted to meet your particular needs and those of the child whom you are teaching, well and good; but you will certainly need to be flexible in your approach and you may well decide to depart in all sorts of ways from the suggestions made here. With dyslexic children one is forced to proceed to a large extent by trial and error, and it seems to me wrong to be tied to one particular method.

Here, then, are some suggestions for your consideration.

1 Ask yourself what the child feels about it all

This seems to me enormously important. By the time a child has been recognised as dyslexic he will already appreciate—vaguely or clearly—that somehow he has failed, that somehow something has gone wrong. In what follows I am thinking mainly of the eight to fourteen age group, since dyslexia is unlikely to be detected before the age of eight, and those over fourteen will already have had years of struggling and frustration behind them. Let us consider the situation before the diagnosis is made. Even when the teachers have been completely humane, he is likely to feel puzzled and bewildered. No doubt we are wrong to over-value literacy, but the fact remains that in our present society people are severely handicapped without it. Often, perhaps, the child has been shown a word and shortly afterwards has failed to recognise it. The 'obvious' inference—if one knows nothing of dyslexia—is that he is not trying or perhaps even wants to be a nuisance. In some cases I have heard of unpleasant family tensions arising from dyslexia—the child going out of the room and slamming the door, for instance, because no one understands him. From his own point of view he knows that there is something which he cannot do, yet clearly other children can do it, and the adults are expecting the same of him. What presumably must add to his dismay is that he *has no idea what it is* that he cannot do. He is almost certain to assume that it is his fault, even if he does not make this assumption explicit.

In many cases, once it is appreciated by the child, the parents and the teachers that there is a specific disability, this kind of tension may well disappear. You should not be surprised, however, if some dyslexic children show in the early stages a sense of defeat and some resistance to being taught. By taking them slowly and giving them reading and spelling tasks that are well within their capability, you are likely to give them the requisite encouragement. Above all, if you show them that you understand something about their disability and that you are not surprised that they feel frustrated, you will be creating the conditions in which it is easier for them to learn.

2 Change your standards of what is easy and difficult

What is easy for normal children may well be very difficult for dyslexic children. It follows that you will need to adjust your standards of when to praise and when to find fault or express concern.

Personally I am a great believer in praise rather than blame—in commending children for what they do well rather than emphasising where they have gone wrong. But one owes it to the child to make clear what one expects of him. A home or school where the child is free to do just as he pleases seems to me undesirable as well as unworkable in practice; one is in effect saying to the child, 'I don't *care* whether or not you saw the legs off the piano; I don't *care* whether or not you hurt the cat.' It seems to me perfectly possible, without reverting to old-fashioned authoritarian methods, to make clear that one *does* care. So, without suggesting that one should 'blame' children in any harsh sense, I am sure one owes it to them to comment on how well or badly they are doing.

Now it seems to me clear that, if a dyslexic child fails at the spelling of an irregular word, or if he correctly applies the rules

19

which you have given him but the particular word happens to be spelled differently, any form of adverse criticism is out of place. If, however, he fails to do what *by his standards* is perfectly possible for him, admonition of the form, 'You can do this if you try,' seems perfectly appropriate. Even so, perhaps one should be careful, since for several years others will have been saying to him, 'You can do it if you try,' in situations where he has tried very hard and yet still been unsuccessful.

The more you can appreciate what he can do and cannot do, the more he will trust you as someone sympathetic to his difficulties. Mutual trust and sound teaching methods seem to me to be essential in the teaching of dyslexic children; and if you employ sound teaching methods, this will help to generate mutual trust.

Sometimes, incidentally, there may be the situation where you have a dyslexic child in your class for, say, geography, but where he is receiving tuition in reading and spelling from someone else. In these circumstances it is perhaps confusing to the child if you attempt to do too much by way of correcting spelling mistakes (and adverse criticism is of course likely to be very disheartening); on the other hand you may feel that really bad spelling should not just be ignored. One possibility might be to say, perhaps in a semi-jocular way, something like: 'I see you still can't spell but I'll leave the spelling, as Mr — is teaching you, isn't he?' This conveys that you understand his difficulty, but avoids giving the impression that you do not care. Of course if you can genuinely say, 'Your spelling has improved,' this may encourage him all the more, though false reassurance seems to me harmful, since if he is in fact not making any progress he is sure to be aware of the fact.

3 Start with regular words and get the child to learn what to do by following rules

The English language is of course very tiresome in the number of irregular words that it contains. You may find with older children that they have a smattering of irregular words and are sometimes surprisingly weak on the regular ones. Very probably they may not be aware of any special difference between regularity and irregularity, except in so far as they *remember* a previous teacher telling them that such and such a word is particularly difficult. One of the most discouraging things is the prospect of having to learn the spelling of each word individually, and it is important to emphasise early on that there are many regularities.

You will probably find, even in the more severe cases, that they can read and spell the very obvious words such as 'the' (though do not be dismayed if words which seem to *you* obvious are not obvious to them). But it will clearly be difficult for the child to

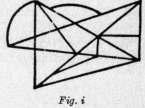

Fig. i

learn any large number of words by this means. If you look at the following pattern (Fig. i) for a brief instant, you may well have considerable difficulty in reproducing it correctly. Unless you know Hebrew the same will be true in the case of Fig. ii.

Fig. ii   מ ד ב ר

If, however, you look at Fig. iii, you will be able to reproduce it at once,

Fig. iii   *enough*

just as those familiar with Hebrew are easily able to reproduce Fig. ii, which is the Hebrew word for 'wilderness'. The point of showing you Fig i and Fig. ii and then showing you Fig. iii for comparison is to exhibit the difference between those marks on paper which are meaningful and those which are not. For the dyslexic child—at least in the early stages—there is no such contrast; all marks on paper beyond a certain degree of complexity are equally meaningless. Now in your own case, if you had sufficient incentive—and I am sure this incentive would need to be very large!—you might be willing to learn the full intricacies of Fig. i by heart, and perhaps a few more figures of similar complexity. But imagine yourself being required to learn a thousand such shapes! In point of fact, since you are lucky enough not to be dyslexic, those shapes which we call *words* are meaningful to you, and you can correctly reproduce (or 'spell') not a thousand but perhaps forty thousand or more of them. It is a sobering thought, however, that by requiring a dyslexic child to learn by heart even fifty words, you would be setting him a task which is as difficult for him as the learning of fifty shapes like Fig. i or Fig. ii would be to you.

This is why the dyslexic child needs to be given *rules*; both for his reading and for his spelling. Only if he has rules can the complexities of the situation be reduced to something manageable.

CHAPTER FIVE

On dividing out the time

To what extent in remedial teaching sessions should one concentrate on reading and to what extent on spelling?

To answer this question we need to consider more fully just what it is that the dyslexic child cannot do.

I have known no dyslexic children who have failed to identify or write down single letters. Presumably in the case of single letters the overall shape is never sufficiently complex to make this task difficult. Thus if presented with the visual marks *a*, *b*, *c*, etc, they are able to make the appropriate noise, whether *ay-bee-see* or *ah-ber-ker*; and if someone else makes one or more of these noises they are able both to imitate what was said and to make the correct marks on paper. They seldom have any severe difficulty if they are told, either visually or auditorily,

what letters to write down. If, however, they are presented with
the set of visual marks which we call a *word*, even though they
can copy this word correctly (i.e. make the right marks on
paper), they may be unable to make the right noise; this is what
we call *being unable to read*. Similarly, if presented auditorily
with the set of sounds which we call a word, even though they
can say the word (i.e. make the right noises vocally), they may
be unable to make the right marks on paper; this is what we
call *being unable to spell*.

Now I have frequently been asked, What happens if dyslexic
children are confronted with *their own* bizarre spelling? My
experience is that they are quite unable to read it, in the sense
of responding specifically to the writing as such, though sometimes they can remember what they were trying to say. (This
ability to remember the right words with minimal inspection of
what is written is sometimes called *barking at print*. It is no
substitute for reading, since the same words will be unrecognised
when presented on a different occasion.) There is no sign, however, that what they have written seems any more bizarre to
them than does any other word which they cannot read. Also I
have usually found in the early stages that they are not
specially troubled—as you or I would be—by the look of a word
which contains several corrections; I frequently have to ask
them to 'start again' instead of correcting the individual letters.
Thus if a dyslexic child wrote *preach* as *peash*, his corrected
effort might be ꬖꬦ. To us this is more uncomfortable to
read than *preach*, although to the dyslexic child there would
be little difference. If, when you are teaching spelling, you
encourage him to look letter by letter at what he has written,
this will have the incidental effect of helping with his reading;
and in some cases, particularly if he has awkward, cramped
writing, it may encourage him to write more clearly.

All this goes to show the subtle ways in which reading and
spelling are interrelated. In particular, if a child is to be able
to spell correctly, he needs to monitor what he has written; in
other words, what he has written needs to be read! If, as part

of his training in spelling he is given practice at such monitoring, this will force him to look more carefully at the details and organisation of the letters; in other words, if things turn out successfully, he will learn to read in the process of being taught to spell.

The *phonetic cues* method which I describe in Chapter 6 aims at achieving precisely this. Although it can be thought of primarily as a method for teaching spelling, my intention is to try to improve the child's reading in the process.

In addition it is possible to give the child what may be called 'straight' reading, that is, to ask him to read aloud from a book and to give him whatever help seems necessary.

Individual cases vary; but if I had a child for sessions lasting fifty minutes, I might well spend, say, ten minutes of the session on general discussion (not necessarily at the beginning), thirty minutes on the *phonetic cues* method, and ten minutes at the end on 'straight' reading.

Although most of the rest of this booklet is concerned with the *phonetic cues* method, I certainly do not wish to give the impression that the other two parts of the session, *viz* general discussion with the child and 'straight' reading, are unimportant; and in the remainder of this chapter I should like to offer some brief comments on each.

With regard to general discussion it is of course enormously helpful if the child is able to be articulate about where his difficulties lie. Also some children are glad to talk about matters not specifically connected with their disability, and I am sure that this should be encouraged. I am not saying that a good relationship between teacher and pupil can on its own cure dyslexia, but I do not doubt that the remedial measures will be more effective if the teacher and pupil really get to know each other. I have perhaps been lucky in that most of the children who have come to me have been very keen to overcome their disability. In the case of the less keen child, one can perhaps discuss with him the reasons which make him reluctant to try to learn; and if these reasons are connected with repeated failure and discouragement in the past, it is possible that a genuine taste of success (even if only very easy words are involved) may convince him that the effort is worth-while.

With regard to 'straight' reading, the main skill here, it seems to me, is that of knowing when to 'prompt' the child and to what extent. It is clearly necessary to get across to the child that reading can be a real pleasure, and for this reason assistance with some of the key words should often be given without too much delay; if the child has to struggle a long time for each word his understanding and enjoyment of the story itself may suffer. In the case of difficult and irregular words, it is often kinder to give them instantaneously. One of the problems is that of finding suitable books, since to an intelligent child of ten or eleven, books which contain easy enough words are liable to seem somewhat babyish. Fortunately there are now books for older children where the vocabulary is fairly simple but where the stories are reasonably advanced in subject matter.* Also in some cases you may be able to convey to the child that you appreciate that his intellectual level is higher than that of the children for whom the book was originally intended. Thus I sometimes say to older or brighter children, 'I am sorry if this seems a bit childish, but the intention is to make sure that you have a really good grounding in the easy words.'

Dyslexic children when they read often tend to be very inaccurate. Words are sometimes left out and words not in the text are sometimes imported. It seems to me that quite often they are in fact guessing from one or two letters or sometimes from the total context; certainly discrimination of detail seems to be extra difficult for them. Now the English language is such that guesses of this kind may quite often be successful. There is the risk, however, that some of the guesses will be very wild and that a key word, wrongly recognised, may lead the child off on quite a false trail. I remember a particularly intelligent

* I recommend in particular the *Pathfinder* series by John and Peggy Bradley (Oliver and Boyd), the *Adventures in Reading* series (also *New Adventures in Reading*) by Gertrude Keir (Oxford University Press), and *The Story Path to Reading* series by L. F. Hobley and P. H. Leyden (Blackie and Son Ltd, London and Glasgow).

boy who used this method. His guesses were invariably reasonable ones even when not correct; and he had acquired the
technique of going at a great pace, presumably in the hope that,
if he was somewhere near right, his teacher would not be
strong-minded enough to pull him up! Now I think it is true
that the more fluent one is as a reader the less one has to look
at the letters, or even individual words, in detail. In the early
stages, however, it seems to me that it is right to discourage the
child from too many wild guesses, provided you do not destroy
the enjoyment of the story by continually insisting on full
accuracy.

It may also be helpful, in some cases, to let the child use a
strip of cardboard, laid vertically, as a screen for shutting off
letters other than the ones which he is looking at. I suspect, too
(though I have not the detailed evidence), that dyslexic
children are specially prone to losing the place and 'skipping'
a line; and if your child has this difficulty, a different strip of
cardboard, this time laid horizontally across the width of the
page, may make things easier for him.

One final problem in connection with reading requires mention, that of whether the method of *look-and-say* is likely to be
helpful with dyslexic children. When this method is used the
child is required in the first place to look at the word as a whole
and to recognise it as a whole, without concerning himself until
later over the details of individual letters. Thus reading books
which use this method might early on present the child with a
long word, such as *aeroplane*, on the grounds that such a word
is so distinctive that it could easily be recognised on a later
occasion. The contrasting method is the *phonic* method, in
which the child is required to sound the individual letters and
hence build up the complete word; here it is usual to start with
short regular words, e.g. cat, sat, etc.

Now the method which I shall describe is in fact a variant of
the phonic method, and I am in no doubt that, for the great
majority of dyslexic children, the phonic method in some form
or another, rather than *look-and-say*, is likely to be the more
effective. This, indeed, is what one might expect from the very

nature of dyslexia. These children, one should remember, have been described as *word-blind* (compare p. 6). For them the look of a word, unless they are very familiar with it, does not make sense, and where it does not make sense at a first glance there is no good reason to suppose that a second or third look at it will improve matters. If the child is put under pressure and told to try harder, he may simply *stare* harder, and this will probably make things worse. You have perhaps yourself experienced the curious feeling which sometimes arises if a word is repeated over and over again: it tends to lose its meaning and becomes just a sound. A similar effect can also be produced if you stare at print: what was a meaningful word becomes mere marks on paper. It is difficult for us to put ourselves in the position of the dyslexic child; but I suspect that this feeling, after a period of repetition or staring, that the word has *lost its meaning* gives us a temporary and fleeting awareness of something which for dyslexics is permanently present.

It is possible, however, that there may be a minority of dyslexic children for whom the *look-and-say* method is helpful. Although in most cases of dyslexia one of the main difficulties is that *visual* marks (i.e. letters and words) do not convey meaning, you may occasionally come across children for whom the problem is primarily *auditory* rather than visual, and in these cases it is sounds rather than visual shapes which tend to be confused or put in the wrong order. If the visual marks do not present particular difficulty, there is obviously a greater likelihood that the method of *look-and-say* will be successful. On the whole, however, as far as dyslexic children are concerned, I am opposed to it.

CHAPTER SIX

Building the dictionary

Introductory comments

The method which I shall describe in this chapter (the *phonetic cues* method) is intended to use with children whose speech, eyesight and hearing are fairly normal and who can name and write individual letters of the alphabet, but who in both reading and spelling have difficulty in combining letters to make a word.

I do not wish to claim any great originality for it;* still less do I wish to claim that I have *the* answer to the problem of dyslexia. My purpose, as I have repeatedly made clear, is simply to make a few tentative suggestions which can be adapted to suit individual needs.

One of the main features of the method is that the child should say the word very carefully and should pay special attention to the movements of his tongue, lips and throat in doing so. He is already able to repeat words correctly (except in some cases for awkward polysyllabic words), and though he cannot pass directly from hearing the word or saying it to writing the whole word down, he can pass from saying a part of it, e.g. the first letter, to writing that first letter down, and so build the word up from the movements of tongue, lips and throat which he makes in saying the successive letters.† The important thing here is that one is giving the child rules to

---

* Among other books which make special use of the phonic approach I should like to mention in particular *Sounds and Words* (Books 1–6) by V. Southgate and J. Havenhand (University of London Press Ltd). Although not explicitly designed for dyslexic children, these volumes could well form a useful adjunct to the present booklet.

† Some dyslexic children may, of course, have difficulty in arranging letters in the *correct* succession, and in these cases it is inadvisable to introduce longer words too early.

follow. I remember one boy who described his spelling difficulty succinctly and correctly by saying, 'I don't know what letter to put next.' This is just the problem. Without rules the child simply does not know what to do.

As has been pointed out (p. 7), the spelling of dyslexic children is often *phonetic* in character. Here are some further examples: *auva* for *over*, *sissder* for *sister*, *disdns* for *distance* and *icksatley* for *exactly*. I have often found this kind of misspelling in school exercise books before I myself started to teach the child. This suggests that some dyslexic children may implicitly be using the method of *phonetic cues* even before it is explained to them. If this is so, one's job is to make them explicitly aware of what they are doing, to encourage them to continue with the method, and to point out possible pitfalls.

i The first page

For the first lesson the child should be asked to bring a new exercise book. This will serve as his *dictionary*. In what follows I shall indicate ways in which the dictionary can gradually be built up. An example of a completed dictionary is given in Chapter 7.

I have found it convenient to start with regular three-letter words having a vowel in the middle and a consonant at each end. With words of this kind the main source of difficulty for dyslexic children is the vowel, and I therefore arrange for the first page of the dictionary to be divided up into five columns, one for each of the short vowels, *ă*, *ĕ*, *ĭ*, *ŏ*, and *ŭ*.* I start him off with the words *bag*, *beg*, *big*, *bog*, and *bug*; and I ask him to write these five words across the page, pointing out to him that they are the same except for the vowel in the middle. Incidentally, although I have usually found that the child knows what a vowel is, you would be wise to check on this. The same applies

* In what follows I use the symbol ˘ over a vowel to indicate a short vowel and the symbol – to indicate a long vowel. Thus the *a* in *tap* is short and would be written *ă*; the *a* in *tape* is long and would be written *ā*. It is not, of course, necessary to introduce the child to this notation, since you will be presenting the material to him auditorily.

to other terms which may come up in later lessons. These may sometimes be so familiar to oneself that one is apt to overlook the fact that others may find them baffling. In general it is most important in teaching dyslexic children to take nothing for granted, however intelligent they may seem in some respects.

The next thing is to tell the child to make the *noises*. I have come to use *noise* almost as a technical term. It means the vowel sound. Thus the *noise* for *bag* is ă. It is often helpful at the start if you say ă, ĕ ĭ, ŏ, ŭ and ask him to imitate you. It is worth remembering that vowel sounds vary somewhat in different localities, and I suggest that you adjust your vowel sounds to get them as near as possible to those of the child.

Next call his attention to the fact that ă is the *noise* for *bag*. 'Say *bag*; now say *ag*; now say ă.' Tell him to note what he does in his throat when he says ă, and tell him that whenever he does this in his throat the right vowel is *a*.* Repeat for *beg*, *big*, *bog* and *bug*. In my experience the ĭ *noise* is the easiest to differentiate, with the ŏ *noise* next.

Then continue: 'Here are some more words with the noise ă. Put them in the ă column. Don't forget that because the noise is ă you must write the letter *a*. *Sat* . . . *hat* . . . *rat* . . . *mat* . . . *map* . . . Now here are some words with the noise ĕ. Put them in the ĕ column. Don't forget that because the noise is ĕ you must write the letter *e*. *Set* . . . *met* . . . *pet* . . . *ten* . . . *hen*.' You should then carry on in a similar way for ĭ, ŏ and ŭ. When the child has grasped the principle, tell him that *he* must now say which column the word goes in. If he has difficulty tell him to make the *noise* first and to note how he moves his throat in doing so. The *noise* can be obtained by cutting off the first letter and then the third, e.g. *met*, *et*, ĕ. Note that when the child is

---

* Where the symbols ⌄ and – are not used I am of course referring to the *name* of the letter as opposed to its *noise*. You will probably wish to pronounce this vowel *ay* (to rhyme with *may*) unless the child is so familiar with the *ah-ber-ker* pronunciation that it seems best not to change him over. It is advisable to find out the child's preference at an early stage, and once a pronunciation has been agreed you will obviously want to keep to it.

asked to spell, e.g. *map*, after being given *rat* and *mat*, the task is slightly different, since he has to vary the final consonant instead of the first one. As soon as he can manage this with no difficulty, he should be given three-letter words where both consonants have to be varied.

At a suitable point you may like to introduce words which have two consonants, e.g. *trap, flat, drop*, etc. In the early stages do not vary the consonants too much; thus if he has just been given *drop*, this is a good time to ask him to spell *crop* and *prop*. Also, with suitable warning about change of column, you may like to follow *drop* with *drip*. (Do not overload the child by giving him too much to think about at once.) When the child is used to words with two consonants in succession, try words with three consonants in succession, e.g. *strip, strap, split*. It is often helpful to lead up to these words gradually; thus *strip* could follow *trip*, *strap* could follow *trap*, and *split* could follow *lit* and *slit*.

At a convenient time (not necessarily very early on) you may like to introduce two-letter words having the same noises but with no consonant at the start; thus *at* can join *sat* and *hat*, *up* can join *cup*, and *on* can join *dot*. In this last case a word spelled *blank-o-n* would have eased the transition, but there is no suitable word. (*Con* or *don* would have done, but they are unlikely to be sufficiently familiar to the child to justify inclusion at this stage.)

After the initial explanations you should continue to build up the first page of the dictionary, adding to it on successive lessons as the child meets new words which 'fit' particular columns.

Towards the end of the first lesson—or at some other fairly early stage—you may like to give the child a dictation. Possible exercises are given on p. 52 *seq*. These exercises can be interrupted at any time if it seems a convenient moment to add new words to the dictionary.

I should like to conclude this section with some general remarks which may also be applicable when later pages of the dictionary are being built up.

The first point concerns the use of the exercises given in Chapter 8. No exercise should be given until the child has been introduced to the appropriate *noises*. The exercises have in fact been numbered in such a way that they indicate what pages of the dictionary are being tested. Thus exercises 4A and 4B assume that he has been introduced to all the *noises* as far as page 4 of the dictionary. There are two special reasons why it is important not to ask him to spell words for which he has not been given the rules. In the first place, by including the word in a dictation test, you are thereby implying that you expect him to know it. Since he is dyslexic, however, he will almost certainly *not* know it, and you are therefore showing no more understanding of his condition than his earlier teachers who knew nothing of dyslexia. Secondly, the whole point of the method is to convey to him that, if he follows the rules, he can deduce what letters to put next. One needs to explain that some words are awkward and that in these cases rule-following will not help; but such words can be deferred until his confidence has been built up. If he is given regular words he can discover for himself that he is being successful; and, conversely, if through slackness or bewilderment he fails to follow the rules, he will discover that he has made mistakes. These are mistakes which he could have avoided. If he makes them, you can indicate that you expect him to do better; but it is futile to expect a dyslexic child to spell a word unless he has been told how to set about doing so, and you will only increase his bewilderment. Both teacher and child need to be clear which words the child is expected to spell and which not.

This does not mean that unfamiliar words should never be given. Thus if he has been introduced to the ō *noise*, as in *goat* and *boat*, it is perfectly in order to give him the word *stoat* even if he has never seen it spelled before. You will notice that plenty of words are included in the exercises which are not in the specimen dictionary. All of them, however, are words to whose *noises* the child has been introduced. They can of course be added to the dictionary whenever this seems convenient, and in each case the child should be required to say which is the correct column for them (or, as he might prefer to say, what words they 'go with' or what words 'belong in the same family'). If, as happens in some cases, the child does not understand the idea of a 'rhyme', he may have some initial difficulty in recognising that words go in 'families'; but in my experience this can be overcome with practice.

Where a word is regular but unfamiliar, the sort of thing which one can say is, 'Make the *noise* first; you can do this word if you stick to the rules.' Indeed, one of the skills which you are trying to teach him is how to tackle new words. There is, of course, no need to wait until a particular page of the dictionary is *complete* before the exercises are given; fresh words—provided they satisfy the rules—can continually be added.

If the child is writing something for himself—a letter to one of his family, perhaps—and if he needs words which are irregular or for which he has not yet been given the rules, it is probably best to tell him the correct spelling at once rather than spend time on it. Thus if the word were *laugh* one might say, 'That's difficult and I'll give it to you—*l-a-u-g-h*', rather than see if he knows it (which is most unlikely) or try to get him to apply rules (which in this case is impossible).

I have assumed in the exercises that the child has already learned, or will soon pick up, the following nine words: *I*, *a*, *the*, *he*, *she*, *or*, *be*, *me* and *and*. *No other word has been taken for granted*. In the case of all other words they must either be built up in accordance with specified rules or else individually noted as exceptions.

There is no reason why you should not invent your own dictation exercises; but you should remember that even easy words (i.e. words which seem easy to us) present difficulty to a dyslexic child.

A further question is, what should one do if the child continually *reverses* letters, e.g. if he confuses *b* and *d* or *p* and *q*. I do not know of any really satisfactory short cut for eliminating this kind of mistake, though it is sometimes said that asking the child to trace the letter 'in the air' may help him, and many teachers have their own special mnemonics. At the very least, it seems to me, one should call the child's attention to his mistake so that he can correct it, though it is very important, of course, to make clear that one expects this kind of mistake and appreciates his difficulty. Detailed evidence is scanty, but I think it likely that most dyslexic children will gradually manage to stop *reversing*, though they may slip back into their old habits if they are under stress or in a great hurry.

Another point of importance is that, in the early stages at least, you should not include words which, though they have the required letters, do not involve the right *noise*. Thus, although *on* can be included with *pot*, *not* etc. in the fourth column of page 1 of the dictionary, it would be muddling if you also included e.g. *son*, *ton or won*. Similarly it would be muddling if, in column 1 of page 2 of the dictionary, along with *gave* and *wave*, you also included *have*. Minor variants can be assimilated by most children; thus the inclusion of *again* next to *pain* and *rain* or the inclusion of *aloud* next to *loud* is unlikely to cause confusion provided you call their attention to the *a* at the start. Similarly words with the extra *n* before the *d*, e.g. *sound* and *found*, can be included in the same column as *loud* without too much difficulty. But if you introduce major variants (e.g. if you followed *sound* by *mountain* on the grounds that this, too, had *o-u*) you will be making things too complicated. What the child needs is simplicity.

I have, however, permitted myself one exception. I have called the final page of the dictionary, 'Some special groups'; and here I have included words which 'go together' for various reasons, not connected with the *noise*, e.g. months of the year, the *o-u-g-h* words, and words beginning with *k-n*. That *though*, *cough* etc. all have *o-u-g-h* DESPITE not sounding the same is an idea which the child may grasp later on, and at this later stage associating these words may help him. In the early stages, however, complications of this kind should be avoided.

ii The second page

In the case of bright children it is usually possible to introduce the second page at the start of the second lesson; but you will of course have to adjust your speed to the needs of the particular child whom you are teaching.

'Last time I showed you the five noises ă, ĕ, ĭ, ŏ, ŭ. Would you like to say them over again to make sure you remember them? . . . Now I am going to introduce you to some new noises, namely ā, ī and ō. You have already met the words *mat*, *pip*, and *not*, with noises ă, ĭ, and ŏ. Now I am going to introduce you to the words *mate*, *pipe* and *note*. *Mat* is *m-a-t*; *mate* is *m-a-t-e*. *Pip* is *p-i-p*; *pipe* is *p-i-p-e*. *Not* is *n-o-t*; *note* is *n-o-t-e*. In each case you have to add an *e*. Where you add an *e* it turns ă into ā, ĭ into ī, and ŏ into ō. Write down *mate*, *pipe* and *note* in your dictionary . . . Now spell the following words and put them in the right column of your dictionary; *late* . . . *date* . . . *hate* . . . *plate* . . . *came* . . . *same* . . . *wipe* . . . *ripe* . . . *tripe* . . . *stripe* . . . *time* . . . *mine* . . . *nine* . . . *home* . . . *joke* . . . *poke* . . . *spoke* . . . *stroke* . . . *page* . . . *rage* . . . *hope* . . . *ride*.'

As soon as the child has grasped what is required, it is helpful to vary the columns at random, as is done from *stroke* onwards. With regard to double and triple consonants, you will notice in the above list that *ripe* was followed by *tripe* and *stripe*. At a later stage double and triple consonants can be mixed at random with single ones (compare p. 31).

If you use the *ay-bee-see* pronunciation when referring to the names of letters, it will probably help to point out that where the final (or 'lazy') *e* is present the correct *noise* for the main vowel is also that vowel's name.

This page of the dictionary has only three columns, in contrast with the five on the first page. This is because *a*, *i* and *o* are the vowels which most commonly lengthen when a final *e* is added. There are a few words where the *u* lengthens, e.g. *tune* and *mute*, but these seem to me to be too few and infrequent to justify inclusion at this stage. A further difficulty is that the *u* in *u-blank-e* is sometimes pronounced *oo*, as in *jute*, *flute* and *fluke*, and this is the kind of extra complication which should certainly not be brought in early on. Similarly there are a few words ending *e-blank-e* where the first *e* is long, e.g. *theme*, but they are mostly unusual words and in some cases there is danger of confusion with other words which sound the same but are spelled differently; thus *deme* might be confused with *deem* and *mete* with *meet* or *meat*. Since the long *e* is far more commonly represented by *ee* or *ea*, it seems an unnecessary complication to introduce *e-blank-e* at this early stage. I have therefore limited this page to the long *a*, the long *i* and the long *o*.

When you have introduced these three *noises*, you may like to try any of the dictation exercises up to number 2B.

iii The third page

'Do you by any chance know the two different ways of spelling *sea*—*sea*—the-water and *see*—what-you-do-with-your-eyes? You do? Good (or, You don't? Never mind). *See*—what-you-do-with-your-eyes—is spelled *s-e-e*; *sea*—the-water is spelled *s-e-a*. Now I am going to introduce you to two different kinds of *e* noise; one is spelled *e-e* like *see*—what-you-do-with-your-eyes, and one is spelled *e-a* like *sea*—the-water. First of all, will you go to page 3 of your dictionary and write down *see*—what-you-do-with-your-eyes . . . *s-e-e*, that's very good. Could you add in brackets the word *eyes*? I will spell it for you as it is difficult, *e-y-e-s*. Now, in the next column, will you write *sea*—the-water? . . . *s-e-a*, that's very good. Now add *water* in brackets, *w-a-t-e-r*.'

Two points arise here. **a** This method of presentation makes clear the difference between words which the child can be expected to spell by obeying the rules and other words which he cannot be expected to spell. *Eyes* and *water* of course come in the latter group. **b** One is frequently confronted with the problem of *homophones*, i.e. words which sound the same but have a different spelling, e.g. *see-sea, meat-meet, been-bean, road-rode*. In the case of the more common words I have found it helpful to write in something (e.g. *eyes* and *water* in the case of *see-sea*) to indicate which member of a pair is which. Since neither *eyes* nor *water* are words which the child is expected to know at this stage, it is therefore futile to waste time asking him to spell them. If the word is one which he *can* spell (e.g. *street* to explain *road*, see p. 37) then of course he should be asked to do it. In some cases (e.g. *pain-pane, main-mane, ail-ale*) you may decide that one member of the pair is rare enough to be ignored. It is, I think, better simply to hope the child will not confuse e.g. *pain* (=ache) with window-*pane*, rather than clutter up his dictionary with too many complications. At this stage one wants the child to be able to spell the words which he will most commonly meet and need; this is more important than trying to safeguard him against mistakes over relatively rare words such as *pane, mane,* or *ail.*

'Here are some words that go *e-e*, like *see*—what-you-do-with-your-eyes: *deep . . . keep . . . seed . . . need . . . feed . . . steep . . . sleep . . . creep . . . green . . . street . . . queen . . .* Here are some words that go *e-a*, like *sea*—the-water: *eat . . . seat . . . beat . . . heat . . . read. . . pea . . . tea . . . heap . . . leap . . . cheap . . . speak.* Now whenever you meet the ē noise, you can be pretty sure the spelling will be either *e-a* or *e-e*, but, unless you know the words, you won't be able to tell which. You may sometimes have to guess, and if you guess wrongly I shall not mind; it is just bad luck. But with a bit of practice you will remember which words go *e-e* and which go *e-a*. Would you like to read the *e-a* words you've written? . . .'

'Finally here's a puzzling one for you, the word *meat*. If you have *meat* for lunch, it is spelled *m-e-a-t*; if you *meet* someone in the street it is spelled *m-e-e-t*. Put the *meat* for lunch here, and I suggest you put in brackets beside it *food*—I'll spell that for you; it's *f-o-o-d* . . . Put the *meet*-in-the-street here; let us call it *meet-someone*, so put *someone* in brackets—I'll spell it, as it's a difficult word: *s-o-m-e-o-n-e*. As an extra reminder, why not put *street* here? You can spell it yourself; I'll simply tell you it's an *e-e* word.'

When you have introduced words with *e-e* and *e-a*, you may like to try any of the exercises up to number 3B.

iv The fourth page

'Here are some more *noises*. There are two extra complications I want to introduce you to today.' (These can be introduced separately if you think it more suitable.) 'The *ā* noises that I've shown you so far go *a-blank-e*, like *plate* and *date*; and the *ō* noises go *o-blank-e*, like *home* and *poke*. But there's another kind of *ā* noise and another kind of *ō* noise; the other kind of *ā* noise goes *a-i* and the other kind of *ō* noise goes *o-a*. Here are some *ā*-noise words which go *a-i*; you will be able to spell them correctly when I've done the first one: if I wait for you, *wait* is spelled *w-a-i-t*.' (This explanation is included to avoid confusion with *weight*, which is too difficult a word to bring in at this stage.) 'Write it down on p. 4 of your dictionary . . . Now do *nail* . . . *fail* . . . *rain* . . . *pain* . . . *Spain* . . . *stain* . . . *sprain* . . . *strain* . . . *again*. (*Sp*, *spr*, *st* and *str* are deliberately put side by side here. You should encourage the child to differentiate them, going back over each several times if he has difficulty.) '*Again* is like the others but you need to put an *a* at the beginning—an extra *ă* noise.' 'Now here are some *ō*-noise words which go *o-a*: *boat* goes *b-o-a-t*. Write it down in the next column . . . Now do *goat* . . . *load* . . . *foam* . . . *loaf* . . . *oats*; be careful of this one but I think you will be able to do it.' (You should explain the absence of consonant at the start and the *s* at the end if the child has difficulty.) 'Now try the *road* that you walk along . . . *r-o-a-d* . . . good! Now this is the sort of road like a street, so put *street* in brackets, whereas if someone *rode* on a horse you would spell it *r-o-d-e*, like the words with the *ō* noise on your second page.' (It may be convenient to refer back to page 2 of the dictionary at this point and ask the child to add *rode* with *horse* in brackets.)

'Here are some slightly more awkward *a-i* words, because they have an extra *n* in them. *Paint* is spelled *p-a-i-n-t* . . . Now try *faint* . . . Now here's a difficult one, *restraint* . . . Now try *constraint*.' (I think it does no harm to throw in the occasional difficult word, such as this, provided there is some chance of success. In the case of *restraint* the child will be able to get the *r*, and perhaps with prompting could get the *e*, while the rest follows by simply obeying the rules of the current lesson. You should make clear, however, that you regard the word as difficult and that you will not be disappointed if the child fails.

It is, of course, an enormous fillip to *bright* dyslexic children if they find themselves able to spell more sophisticated words, and if one can find sophisticated regular words this may help to keep off boredom.)

'Now I'm afraid you'll just have to *know* which *ā*-words go *a-blank-e* and which go *a-i*. Similarly you'll just have to *know* which *ō*-words go *o-blank-e* and which go *o-a*. But you'll have your dictionary to help you; and quite often, when you are in doubt about a word, you may like to ask yourself, What are the words in the same list?' I have found that if the child is in difficulty and I ask (or get him to ask himself) about the words that 'go with' a particular word, as e.g. *pain* goes with *rain*, this sometimes helps him to remember.

When you have introduced words with *a-i* and *o-a* you may find it helpful to try any of the exercises up to number 4B.

v The fifth page

'Now I want you to make page 5 of your dictionary a special page in which you put all the irregular, difficult words. English is a difficult language; in fact that's one of the reasons why you have had special difficulty with your reading and spelling. If you follow the rules I've given you, you will be able to spell quite a lot of words right; but there are some tiresome ones where there aren't any rules, and in these cases there's no short cut—you simply have to know them.

'Let us put some of these awkward ones in your dictionary. I'll start with *father*; it is *f-a-t-h-e-r*. . . . *Mother* is similar, but instead of *f-a* you put *m-o*. . . . The *sun* in the sky is regular; it is an ordinary *ŭ* noise, so you can turn back and write *sun* among the *ŭ* noises on page one; but *son*, the boy, is spelled *s-o-n*. . . . Let us put *boy* in brackets. . . . *Daughter* is difficult; it has a *g-h* in the middle—*d-a-u-g-h-t-e-r*.'

Similar explanations can be made when the other groups of words are introduced. (For details of the grouping see p. 45, i.e. p. 5 of the dictionary.) Words in each group can be recognised as 'belonging together' in some way or other, and the extra *contextual* information may conceivably be of help, especially in the groups *here, there, where* and *should, could, would*. I do not advise introducing more than about two groups in any one session.

A knowledge of the words in groups **i** to **v** is assumed from exercise 5A onwards, and a knowledge of the words in groups **vi** to **xi** is assumed from exercise 9A onwards.

This seems a convenient point to give a thumb-nail sketch of the method in action. You may not ever meet the particular mistakes mentioned here; but if you meet similar mistakes—as you are sure to do—you may like to know the kind of comments which I myself have thought it helpful to make.

Let us suppose, then, that when asked to spell *stoat* the child spells it *strot*. In the first place, let us try to discover his reasoning. In occasional cases, due perhaps to confusion, tiredness, or lack of effort, there is no reasoning to be found, but this is rare. In this case he has been careless and confused $\bar{o}$ and $\breve{o}$; he has also become tangled with the consonants at the start, and has tried to remedy the situation by including the superfluous *r* (perhaps because he was earlier told to put it in when he misspelled *sprig* as *spig*). Here are some suggested comments: 'Look, you are being careless. What's the *noise*? . . . Well, say it again—*stoat*; cut off the *ter* at the end, and say *stō*: now cut off the *ster* at the beginning . . . $\bar{o}$—it *must* be. All right, how do we do $\bar{o}$? There are two ways—what are they? . . . You've forgotten. All right; let us look it up.' (Ask him to turn up the correct pages of his dictionary) . . . 'That's right: o-blank-e and o-a. If you don't know which, you'll just have to guess. I don't mind if you guess wrong—which is it? . . . No, bad luck! It's o-a. But in any case you left the *e* out; you in fact put *strŏt*.' (The child cannot *see* that he has put *strŏt*, but you are offering him a way of recognising what he has put, or at any rate are showing him that misspellings cause the reader to make the wrong noise.) '. . . Good, you've altered the *o* to o-a. But you still haven't really been careful. Listen—*stoat, stroat*. Can you hear the difference? You say them. . . . What's the difference? One of them has *s-t-r* and one just has *s-t*. . . . Quite right, this

40

one has *s-t*. Well, now it's all done; you needn't wonder what to put next. You know it is *s-t* at the beginning; you know it is *t* and the end, and you know it is *o-a* in the middle. You hadn't met the word, but you know now how to set about spelling a new word.'

I am not of course suggesting that you should follow this presentation in every detail; clearly each remedial teacher has his own personal 'style'. I hope, however, that the above pieces of conversation will have given you some sort of 'feel' for possible ways of conducting your sessions; and you will of course be able to modify your procedure in the light of experience.

vi Concluding remarks

The previous sections have indicated possible ways of introducing new *noises* and new words; and you will be able to apply the same procedure as you build up the later pages of the dictionary. I need not therefore repeat the same formulae and the same explanations for each fresh page. What I suggest is that you use the sample dictionary on pp. 43 *seq.* as your guide and introduce new pages at whatever pace is most convenient for the child. Once he has been shown the rule, he should be required to spell the fresh word for himself; and his own dictionary will finally look like a manuscript version of the dictionary on pp. 43 *seq.* There is, of course, absolutely no need for it to be an exact replication. There may be many words not included in this book, which you may decide to add, and the brighter children will probably produce examples of their own of words which 'fit' a particular column; thus when shown *drink* and *think* a child might ask if he can add *wink*, and you may even like to play a 'game' with him in which you each add a word alternately. A photostat copy of a page from an actual dictionary is given on page 42. If at the end of your teaching sessions the child is able to spell the majority of words in his dictionary and to recognise them in context during his reading, then, even if he still has difficulty over irregular and more complicated words, at any rate the worst problems and frustrations will be behind him.

Bag ~~bag~~ Bey   Big   Bag   Bug

Bat ~~set~~ Bet   Dig   hag   gun.

cat set leg   Hit   ~~Drop~~ Fun

sad ~~set~~ Bed   Trip   Drop   Sun

cap ~~stem~~ stem   Grip   Crop   Nun

hat   Slip   Prop   Bun

trap   Clip   Stop   Run

tap   Sip   Strop

Slap   Strip

~~sap~~   thin   ~~block~~

clap   thick   block.

that   ~~trick~~   plot.

stack (ck)   brick   ~~dot.~~

sock.   Lick   ~~spot.~~

spat.   stick.   rot.

sat.   prig.   trot.

flat   sprig

~~fat~~ fat.

vat.

can

~~they~~

CHAPTER SEVEN

A sample dictionary

Page 1 The ă, ĕ, ĭ, ŏ, and ŭ noises

bag	beg	big	bog	bug
sat	met	pig	fog	rug
hat	get	fig	log	jug
rat	pet	sit	hot	hut
mat	ten	bit	pot	bun
map	men	hit	dot	cup
at		it	on	up
trap	step	drip	drop	shut
strap	hen	trip	crop	
clap	then	strip	prop	
flap	when	split	flop	
flat		clip	stop	
shall	bell	hill	doll	gull
	well	fill		
		stiff	off	stuff
		sniff		cuff
mass	mess	miss	cross	fuss
	less	kiss	loss	
sack	peck	pick	shock	suck
back	neck	sick	clock	duck
pack	deck	lick	rock	stuck

Note. If the pupil finds this page easy you may like to introduce the words given on p. 48 before proceeding further. When later you reach p. 48, p. 43 should in any case be studied in conjunction with it.

Page 2 The *ā*, *ī*, *ō* noises with final *e*

mate	pipe	note
late	wipe	home
date	ripe	joke
hate	tripe	poke
plate	stripe	spoke
came	time	stroke
same	mine	hope
page	nine	rose
rage	ride	rode (horse)

Page 3 The *ē* noises (*e-e* and *e-a*).

see (eyes)	sea (water)
deep	eat
keep	seat
seed	beat
need	heat
feed	read
steep	pea
sleep	tea
creep	heap
green	leap
street	meat (food)
queen	bean (food)
meet (someone)	cheap
been (somewhere)	speak
week (seven days)	weak (not strong)
feel	beam
screen	dream
creak	*creak*
cheep	*cheap*

Page 4 The *a* and *o* noises with no final *e* (-*āi* and -*ōa*)

rain	boat
train	goat
pain	coat
Spain	throat
stain	oats
sprain	road (street)
strain	load
again	loaf
obtain	foam
explain	coach
nail	oak
fail	soak
paint	
faint	

Page 5 Irregular words

i	**ii**	**iii**
father	here	is
mother	there	are
son (boy)	where	was
		were

iv	**v**
he	her
she	their
you	our
they	your

vi	**vii**	**viii**
what	one (once)	said
which	two (to, too)	saw
who	three	some
why	four (for)	come

ix	**x**	**xi**
cause	should	go
because	could	no
please	would	do
have	any	Mr
has	many	Mrs

Page 6 *-oo, -ou,* and *-oi*

soon	loud	boil	look
noon	aloud	toil	cook
stoop	shout	join	hook
boot	spout	coin	foot
tool	found	coil	good
room	sound	avoid	
	ground	*soil*	
	pound	*foil*	
	round	*oil*	

NB soup

Page 7 *-ow, -ay, -oy* and *-y*

cow	say	boy	by	pie
now	may	toy	my	die
how	day	joy	cry	lie
brown	way	annoy	fly	tie
town	pay		dry	
owl	stay		fry	
howl	spray		try	
frown	stray		sky	
scowl	lay		spy	
crown	bay			
down	hay			
	play			
	tray			
	ray			

46

Page 8 *-aught, -ought and -ight*

taught	bought	night
caught	fought	light
daughter	ought	fight
naughty	sought	bright
haughty	brought	slight
slaughter	thought	tight
	nought	alight
		fright
		might
		right
		sight
		flight

Page 9 *-ed, -ing and -ly*

	Verb	*Past Tense*	*Participle*	*Adverb*
Series **i**	wait	waited	waiting	sad—sadly
	paint	painted	painting	glad—gladly
	join	joined	joining	bad—badly
	boil	boiled	boiling	faint—faintly
Series **ii**	hate	hated	hating	light—lightly
	wipe	wiped	wiping	bright—brightly
	joke	joked	joking	tame—tamely
Series **iii**	try	tried	trying	happy—happily
	cry	cried	crying	gay—gaily
	die	died	dying	full—fully
	lie	lied	lying	
	stay	stayed	staying	
Series **iv**	clap	clapped	clapping	
	step	stepped	stepping	
	stop	stopped	stopping	
	blot	blotted	blotting	

47

Page 10 More ă, ĕ, ĭ, ŏ and ŭ noises

mash	mesh	fish	cosh	rush
crash	flesh	dish	splosh	crush
smash		wish		hush
splash				
rash				
bank		think		bunk
sank		wink		trunk
drank		brink		drunk
thank		sink		
		drink		
		ink		
bang		thing	long	
sang		sing	song	
rang		bring	along	
			wrong	
			tongs	
ant	went	mint		punt
pants	sent			hunt
	spent			
	lent			
	tent			
land	mend	wind	pond	fund
sand	spend			
catch	fetch	witch	Scotch	hutch
match		pitch		judge
badge	hedge	bridge	lodge	smudge

48

Page 11 Words in -*le* and -*er*

rattle	kettle	little	bottle	puddle
battle	settle	middle		muddle
paddle				
saddle				

matter	better	bitter	hotter	butter
fatter	setter	litter	spotter	gutter
hatter	letter	sitter	trotter	mutter
hammer		dinner	fodder	drummer
stammer		thinner	odder	summer
manner		winner		
spanner		kipper		
		kitten		

Page 12 Other word families: I

ball	bell	will	car	fir	fur
fall	well	fill	far	sir	hurt
wall	tell	still	jar	girl	turn
all	smell	spill	tar	bird	burn
call	spell	till	farm	shirt	purse
hall	sell	pill	harm	skirt	nurse
tall	fell	hill	arm	dirty	curse
stall		drill	cart	first	murder
small		mill	dart	thirsty	
			tart		
			start		
			party		

Page 13 Other word families: **II**

cold	dear	wild	find
told	near	mild	kind
hold	fear	child	mind
fold	hear (ears)		bind
bold	ear		blind
scold	gear		behind
	smear		
	clear		
	appear		

munch	hinge	torch	large
crunch	fringe	arch	forge

beach	stooge	much	rich
coach	gouge	such	which

Page 14 Words in *-tion*

station	position	motion	solution
nation	condition	notion	resolution
relation	ignition	lotion	revolution
indignation	prohibition	promotion	persecution
explanation	recognition		constitution
	opposition		

action
fraction
subtraction
direction
correction
question
prescription
adoption

Page 15 Supplement: some special groups

Monday	January	five	twenty
Tuesday	February	six	thirty
Wednesday	March	seven	forty
Thursday	April	eight	fifty
Friday	May	nine	sixty
Saturday	June	ten	seventy
Sunday	July	eleven	eighty
	August	twelve	ninety
	September	thirteen	a hundred
	October	fourteen	a thousand
	November	fifteen	a million
	December	sixteen	

danger	knight		brother
poison	knee		sister
toilet	knit		aunt
police	know		uncle
	knew		cousin
	knife		nephew
	knock		niece
			grandmother
			grandfather
			friend

dough	through	plough
though		bough
although		

rough	cough	thorough
tough	trough	borough
enough		

51

CHAPTER 8

Exercises

Notes 1 The number given to each exercise represents the corresponding page-number in the dictionary. If more than one exercise is given per page, the exercises are numbered 1A, 1B, etc. All the words in the exercises are words which occur *on or before* the corresponding page in the dictionary; the child is never expected to spell a word if he has not been introduced to its *noise*.

2 It is assumed that the words *I, a, the, he, she, or, be, me* and *and* can already be spelled by the child.

Exercise 1A

1 I had a big pig.
2 Tom had not got a cup.
3 Bob had a red bag.
4 Ron sat in the mud.
5 Can it be Pat?
6 Let him sit on the rug.
7 Get a big mat.
8 I am not hot.
9 The man had got the cod.
10 He did not let the fat dog sit on the mat.

Exercise 1B

1. He did not trip the man up.
2. The hen and the pig sat in Bob's flat.
3. She let the hot log slip on to the step.
4. The brick got stuck in the bog.
5. The duck had bad luck.
6. Tom did not stick in the hut.
7. The pot had a crack in it.
8. The dog ran on; it did not stop.
9. Tom got ten men to tug the pig back.
10. I did not get back to the rock.

Exercise 2A

1. He came home late.
2. The dog did not bite the bone.
3. Pat can bake a cake.
4. He came up nine times.
5. The plate had five cakes on it.
6. Let Bob ride on the dog.
7. I can wade in the lake.
8. The cat bit the tame pig.
9. She hates cats.
10. Mike did not like the red robes.

Exercise 2B

1. He hates it if his dogs get in late.
2. Dad came up to the man and spoke to him.
3. Bob had a red nose.
4. I can hide in the big hole.
5. Tom had a bad time at Mike's home.
6. Note the date.
7. The cat came up the lane.
8. Make him take the cake home.
9. I did not stroke the cat.
10. Tom did not like to smoke a pipe.

Exercise 3A

1 I can see the sea.
2 The dog likes to eat meat.
3 I met Tom in the street.
4 The man in the shop gave Bob a fine set of robes.
5 I need a big stick.
6 Mike came back home and spoke to Jack.
7 The queen came up the street.
8 The red rose is not mine.
9 I need cheap meat from the shop.
10 Can the dog or the cat lead me home?

Exercise 3B

1 I like to be neat and clean for tea.
2 I fed him on sweets and he got fat.
3 Let me see the red rose.
4 Did I drop a sock on the log?
5 Let Mike lead the dog back home.
6 It is hot and I feel slack.
7 I like to see green peas on my plate.
8 I hope Bob bakes me a cake for tea.
9 Tom likes to wade in the deep sea.
10 I met Mike in the dock but did not speak to him.

Exercise 4A
1. The boat was late and I had to wait.
2. Tom came from Spain in the rain.
3. The goat did not eat the oats.
4. Mike ran to Leeds and then ran home again.
5. Let me see the screen.
6. I did not stroke the black cat.
7. It is bad to poke goats.
8. It is time to paint the boat again.
9. I can see a faint green stain.
10. Tom gave Bob a jug of tea and a loaf.

Exercise 4B
1. Ben met a big rat in the road.
2. The man that I met in Leeds had nine cats.
3. Let him paint a green line.
4. Dad eats ham for tea.
5. Keep the dog on a lead.
6. I can feel that the plate is hot.
7. The boat came in late and I did not wait.
8. The dog did not need to be fed.
9. Mum gave Dad tea in a green pot.
10. I like to sit and read.

Exercise 5A* 1 Where is father? He is here.
2 Where is mother? She is there.
3 Where are you, mother? Are you here?
4 They are at their home.
5 Mother came home for tea.
6 Father came home with his son.
7 Your duck sat on the black rock.
8 Your son sat in the sun.
9 Where did your son sit? It was here.
10 Your father and mother were at home.

Exercise 5B 1 Mother made a cake.
2 Father had to wait in the rain.
3 Where is the road to the sea? It is here.
4 There is cheap meat at the shop.
5 A cat has nine lives.
6 Can you see the green tree?
7 Their green boat can sail on the lake.
8 Were you at home when your father came back?
9 Your son was here.
10 Your father was in a deep sleep.

*This exercise assumes a knowledge of the words in groups **i** to **v** on p. 5 of the *dictionary*, not those in groups **vi** to **xi**, for which the first exercise is **9A**.

Exercise 6A

1 I soon found father by the sea.
2 Mother came late.
3 I made a loud sound and Bob came out.
4 It spoils food to boil it in oil.
5 I did not join Mike in Rome.
6 A loud sound came from the hut.
7 A sheep was there; it was stuck.
8 I came out of the room to get a spoon.
9 Mother found oil on the ground.
10 There were nine sheep in the street.

Exercise 6B

1 The boat was a week late.
2 I like red socks.
3 The men came again and I gave them food.
4 Jane was glad to see her father back.
5 The rain did not spoil the crop of beans.
6 Her boots were on the ground.
7 A loud sound came out of the hole.
8 It is time to meet your daughter.
9 There was a loaf by the gate.
10 Where was father? I found him at home.

Exercise 7A

1 The rain came down and Tom did not stay dry.
2 I may try a game in the hay with Ray.
3 The boy had a red and green toy.
4 The brown cow and the pig came to the town.
5 How did you get that jug? Was it from your father?
6 I had a fine time up in the dales.
7 My dog lay on the ground.
8 How can a man ride a cow?
9 It is now time to join Tom in his boat.
10 There is a red hut by the rock.

Exercise 7B

1 He did not say where he had been.
2 The queen came back from the town.
3 I may stay for about nine days.
4 My father's boots are in the green room.
5 I found that Bob's daughter had been to town.
6 There was a big load of hay by the van.
7 I gave the boy beans on a plate.
8 Creep up to the seat and poke his ribs.
9 Our son has been to Spain.
10 Your daughter spoke to the queen in Rome.

Exercise 8A

1 I bought a big pig at this shop.
2 Tom saw a bright light, and it gave him a fright.
3 Your daughter taught me to read.
4 It was a fine sight to see the town.
5 I may try to fly to Rome.
6 He caught his coat on a spike.
7 Your mother found a brown leaf on the ground.
8 It is not right to fight.
9 I brought my nine plates from the town.
10 Sleep at night but try to stay awake in the day.

Exercise 8B
1 You ought not to have bought the pig.
2 Tom was asleep but a loud sound woke him.
3 I taught Mike to drive.
4 Tom caught a crab in a pool.
5 Sam sat down to wait by the boat.
6 A slight sound woke me up at ten o'clock.
7 I hope you can eat tripe.
8 There were nine dogs on the line.
9 But the train was late and did not hit them.
10 I see a shop where there is cheap meat.

Exercise 9A*
1 I was painting the boat for three days.
2 Please, mother, could you come?
3 I am coming soon.
4 I could not join Mr Brown at nine o'clock.
5 Please let me see the boiling oil.
6 Tom did not say why he had come.
7 Father said he had come because he needed nails for his boat.
8 Which way would you like to come, Mrs Jones? Please say.
9 Yes, there are four boys waiting in the room.
10 I stopped eating beans because I was too fat.

* This exercise is the first to include groups **vi** to **xi** of the irregular words on p. 5 of the dictionary.

Exercise 9B
1 I have waited nine days for the boat.
2 Which is the way to Rome?
3 Why do you have to stay away at nights?
4 Please would you take me to the sea?
5 Who is the man in the red coat?
6 Tom is happily eating some peas.
7 Please stop crying and load up the boat.
8 I tried to get my daughter to play but she would not.
9 It was bad luck that you could not meet the queen.
10 Yes, I can come home in a week's time.

Exercise 10A
1 Tom made a big splash as he dived into the pool.
2 I think there were some fish there.
3 Please could you send some cold meat? That would be kind.
4 Tom poked Bob in the ribs for a joke.
5 I have a pink rash on my hand.
6 My daughter drank four cups of cold tea.
7 I can see the lights winking in the town.
8 The cat sank down nine times but came up again.
9 The boat sank as it had too big a load.
10 I did not think it would sink.

Exercise 10B
1 The brown cow stayed by the end of the rock.
2 My mother's frock is green with pink stripes.
3 The wet streets caused my father to slip.
4 Please can I go and paint the boat?
5 I hope Mr Brown can come and sing.
6 There has been rain for four days.
7 Mrs Smith found a red leaf on the ground.
8 The old coat got crushed in the trunk.
9 The sheep lay asleep in the pen.
10 Please keep your spoon on your plate.

Exercise 11A
1 Please boil the kettle.
2 I hope we can have our tea soon.
3 I had a lot of butter for tea and got fatter.
4 Mother and father could not see where the kettle was.
5 It was too late to go for a swim in the lake.
6 Please send a letter home to your daughter at once.
7 I think it is getting hotter.
8 Do you think so too?
9 Tom stepped in the puddle.
10 His feet got wet.

Exercise 11B　1　Please can I have a little butter and a drink of tea?

2　It was not right to spend a pound on cream filling for the cake.

3　It is better to drink from a cup than from a bottle.

4　I caught sight of a bright light by the sea.

5　Please, father, can I have a hammer and some nails?

6　I thought I would try frying the fish in butter.

7　I hate to wait.

8　I have waited too long.

9　I have waited two days because of the rain.

10　Why did you not say that you were going to Rome?

Exercise 11C　1　I met a red duck in the middle of the lake.

2　It said, 'Quack-quack'.

3　That is what ducks say.

4　The sea was hotter today and I could go for a paddle.

5　Please could your father come and mend the TV?

6　I think he could; Mike can go and see if he is free.

7　Do you like kippers for tea?

8　No, thank you; I should like meat and beans.

9　There were no bees here this summer.

10　I saw some cows poking their noses into my shed.

Exercise 12A
1 I hope the ball will not get stuck in the tree.
2 It is a small ball.
3 Will you please keep still?
4 I lent him a pound; I hope he has not spent it.
5 I ran down to the sea as quickly as I could.
6 Mother hunted about for the kettle for a long time.
7 Would you like to come with me to the town?
8 I should be pleased to join you.
9 Can we get back in time for tea?
10 It will be better to stay in town and not rush home.

Exercise 12B
1 Tom lent his father a tent.
2 Please can I have some ink?
3 I have made a blot which I must wipe up.
4 Please wipe your feet.
5 Which is the way to Leeds?
6 I must rush home or I will be late.
7 I should be delighted if you would stay the night.
8 You are quite right.
9 I did not see the need for a rope.
10 Please come and see us again.

Exercise 12C
1. Tom went away happily smoking his pipe.
2. Father did not spill his drink.
3. Are you ill?
4. I hope you get well quickly.
5. My leg will soon be better.
6. The fitter will come later.
7. Jane taught me how to spell.
8. Do not let me stop you from sleeping.
9. Why can cows not spell?
10. They have not the brain.

Exercise 13A
1. I will need to snatch a cold snack for lunch.
2. I do like butter.
3. There was no play in the football match today.
4. I think our side will be the winners.
5. My father spent two days in a punt.
6. He sent a letter home to my mother each day.
7. I should like to go to the beach.
8. There is still no rain.
9. I caught my foot on the hook and it gave me a fright.
10. I did not hear what Jane said; it was not clear.

Exercise 13B
1. Please teach me to read and spell.
2. I had a paddle in the sea but my feet got cold.
3. The old man sat outside his home.
4. 'Have you a match?' he said.
5. When I gave him one he lit his pipe.
6. The hose-pipe will not reach the hut.
7. Look at the book.
8. Two and two make four—is that right?
9. I have such a good time here that I want to stay.
10. Please may I stay for a week?

Exercise 13C

1 Please drop the latch.
2 Father will be late back.
3 He is teaching some boys to play football.
4 I like to play games some of the time.
5 I will give Jane peaches and cream for tea.
6 Will you settle in Rome?
7 No, I wish to be near my son and daughter.
8 It is cold tonight, but the moon is shining brightly.
9 The little kettle is in the back room.
10 All toys should be put away.

Exercise 14A

1 What day is it today? It is Sunday.
2 Why do we sit here in the rain?
3 It is because we like getting wet.
4 On Sunday night my nose seemed to be bleeding.
5 Did you not see the bright red sky?
6 There might be room for your dog at my home.
7 It would be better if he could sleep in the tent.
8 My daughter boiled the kettle for tea.
9 A pip got stuck in my throat.
10 I did not see the man who fought with Tom.

Exercise 14B 1 The clapping did not stop for a long time.
2 I am happy that you can all come back to tea.
3 Do you like your tea weak or strong?
4 I am trying to keep on the right side of the road.
5 My father caught his coat on a spike.
6 You are quite right; he ought to take it to a shop.
7 My son will spend four days away from home.
8 But I am going to stay in because of the rain.
9 The brown owl sat in the tree.
10 Please can I dry my coat by the stove?

Exercise 14C 1 I made an expedition to the station.
2 The nation will find no solution to its problems without a revolution.
3 My father displayed much indignation at the state of the nation.
4 I was in a good position to see my relations in action.
5 I want an explanation. Why have you come home in such a condition?
6 They did their corrections under the teacher's direction.
7 Please send your questions in the post.
8 The boat needs good navigation.
9 I can do addition and subtraction but I find fractions hard.
10 You have displayed much determination.

Suggestions for further reading

You may find it helpful to subscribe to *The Dyslexia Review*, obtainable from The Dyslexia Institute, 133 Gresham Road, Staines, Middlesex. You may also like to write for recent booklets published by the Helen Arkell Dyslexia Centre, 14 Crondace Road, London SW6. There are, in addition, numerous publications on dyslexia available from the Orton Society, 8414 Bellona Lane, Towson, Maryland 21204, U.S.A.

For some very helpful advice on teaching I recommend three papers by G. C. Cotterell which appear in *Assessment and Teaching of Dyslexic Children*, ed. A. W. Franklin and S. Naidoo, published by the Invalid Children's Aid Association and obtainable from Better Books, 11 Springfield Place, Bath. I have also found Miss Cotterell's 'check list of basic sounds' particularly helpful; this is obtainable, along with her phonic reference cards, from Learning Developments Aid, Paper Works, Norwich Road, Wisbech, Cambridgeshire.

Since the present book first appeared in 1970 the literature on dyslexia has grown considerably. In addition to the books mentioned already I should like to refer to:

B. Hornsby and F. Shear, *From Alpha to Omega*. Heinemann, 1975.

Dale R. Jordan, *Dyslexia in the Classroom*. Merrill, Ohio, 1972.

T. R. Miles and Elaine Miles, *More Help for Dyslexic Children*. Methuen Educational Ltd., 1975.

Among the more technical books on dyslexia may be mentioned:

M. Critchley, *The Dyslexic Child*. Heinemann Medical Books Ltd., 1970.

S. Naidoo, *Specific Dyslexia*. Pitman, 1972.

M. D. Vernon, *Reading and its Difficulties*. Cambridge University Press, 1971.

For help or advice

In the event of difficulty you may like to write to The British Dyslexia Association, 18 The Circus, Bath who may be able to put you in touch with your local Dyslexia Association.

Index